BOOKS BY D.S. MARRIOTT

Incognegro (Salt, 2006)
Hoodoo Voodoo (Shearsman, 2008)
The Bloods (Shearsman, 2011)
Duppies (Commune Editions, 2019)

BEFORE WHITENESS

CITY LIGHTS SPOTLIGHT SERIES NO. 21

D.S. MARRIOTT

BEFORE

WHITENESS

CITY LIGHTS

SAN FRANCISCO

CITY LIGHTS SPOTLIGHT
The City Lights Spotlight Series was founded in 2009,
and is edited by Garrett Caples.

Library of Congress Cataloging-in-Publication Data
Names: Marriott, D. S., author.
Title: Before whiteness / D.S. Marriott.
Description: San Francisco : City Lights Books, 2022. | Series: City Lights
spotlight ; no. 21
Identifiers: LCCN 2021044553 | ISBN 9780872868847 (trade paperback)
Classification: LCC PR6063.A6575 B44 2022 | DDC 821/.92--dc23/
eng/20211012
LC record available at https://lccn.loc.gov/2021044553

Cover art: Linette Eunjoo Park, "Untitled (Grenfell)" [detail] (2021), 11" x 14",
charcoal, conte crayon, and eraser on paper.
Copyright © 2021 by Linette Eunjoo Park

The editor would like to thank Norma Cole, Robert Kaufman,
and Linette Eunjoo Park.

City Lights Books are published at the City Lights Bookstore,
261 Columbus Avenue, San Francisco, CA 94133
www.citylights.com

CONTENTS

for the starrish one

BEFORE WHITENESS

THE GHOST OF AVERAGES

1

hard work,
       hard even for a nigga, but not you.
The French grammar,
       lies open on a table
smeared with grease, oil,—
       unfettered by the chains
 opening the mind begins its flight
and maybe, . . .
       who knows. . . .
the harvested cornfields are green, once again,
    a home for what can be reclaimed
           rather than loss, or delusion,
derided by you, Booker,
      as proof the ancient memories lie unredeemed.

There is hard work
        in the school yard.
I am Kunte Kinte on the hill,
the stars torn from the rolling dusk,
        I sit side by side
  with the dark, the unwelcome brown.
Re-read says my father,
        the coal dust lining his eyes
the focus
        for the reprieve of time, the art of discovery,
                for the receipts
of less gnarled hands and feet.
        He used to call me "dee,"
reminders, too, of how missed letters
        are often the most permanent of things
when the tin can spills
        onto the oilcloth near the unopened book
        and he takes deep breaths
on his knees
        reading the seams of coal for "this is not-me."

I wrote his funeral program in *Word*.
     If one day,
     life rains on you
     a similar dereliction and collapse,
          read that French grammar.
And the boy,
pitied for the ever patient, worn-out binding,
     the loneliness and levels of neglect,
gives tithes against his will:
     remember what is valued, the price it gives.
The privilege is reserved for us—
     Each letter blackened
because a wish to live is deeper
  than seams to be mined,
         or eyes darkened by dust.

LOREM IPSUM

Looking at signs these days
        is all I can manage,
    the world adrift in glances
        as if so much flotsam & jetsam
is where it begins
    and what disturbs the eye is the line
        where boredom subsides
            beneath paneled ceilings.
                It is the ground
pywned because of a lifetime,
    when projects burn
        in thrall to new flames,
    and heads roll as if by magic,
        and the revolution feels cheap
because no longer immaculate (especially in summer),
    maybe because the intervals
                    are now much longer, and the signs
        not so easy to read because, like most of us,
they sweat too. The red ones wink at me as I go past.
                Objects are not things.
Among the poplars
        the lynched body does not resemble

an image. Only the other can save us,
  even though he wears funny peasant shoes
and walks like a German. In the cellar,
 a smell of mold and excrement,
and, in the obscure darkness,
the blackened and burnt stumps
of existence. Hard to forget the relief
  of not taking a bath,
 having just gotten reacquainted
  with the swarm inside my crotch.
 Things are not objects.
  I lie down in the rain,
    decked out in my tiredness,
 bound to what must be remembered,
what is absent.
 I reach out my hands but see nothing. . .
In a poem, silence sounds like a gunshot.
To the flame darkness is an offering,
    in the moment
just before something happens. . . .

BLACK SUNLIGHT

From amid a grove of poplars it appears—and perhaps this testifies to how uninspiring the late morning walk had been—a little aspen tree, shimmering in the heat. It was not so long before this that he had set out, with his boxes and pencils, eager to do some drawing. The sun had been scalding, but despite the heat transfixing him, gouging his forehead, the dusty cart road had been easy underfoot, fringed by oaks and box scrubs. It wasn't long before he had come to a turn in the path and saw the tree: black, sickly, ancestral. By presenting itself in this way, close to the cattle wandering deep in the fields, straining to stand upright amid tightly spaced trees where shafts of light fell in a dense bluegreen, it was as if it were performing a courtesy for those passing through. And further, that it should form a stand in such a hot parched landscape suggested to him the most hopeful of signs—a circle of connection, a return. He decided to sit down and draw it. Beside him he placed a jug of water and a basket of strawberries. He felt content. Thoughts of restlessness abated; his mind grew rooted and still. It was as though something inside him were slowly uncoiling, wanting to burst forth into an act of pure attention. He felt himself recede into the present—as if hit by a sudden cold wave. As he begins to draw the tree seems to arrange itself into an image of the eternity he craved rather than the brute emptiness he feared. But close up he sees something that clutches at his heart: something like a shadow, or a delayed pain, a gaze overflowing from the tree. He didn't know what to do with that ardor overflowing from a tree. Or that gaze. Think instead of a mind trembling under its own weight, trying to glimpse its own undoing; then subtract the feeling of something formless surging on the forested floor, waiting to flow back to the source. Or you could imagine that the tree itself, trying to resist the forces that shaped it, had burrowed back into this black mouth. As though it had given up on its treeness—tired at last of its offices, unwilling to be woven from the earth. As though it had misread its own nature, refusing the illusion of its own form. He had engineered the encounter. He had wanted to see the tree free from artifice, whatever that may be. But it did not. It wanted nothing. Nothing at all. Better stop here. Better to simply stand, serving your purpose, waiting for the world to appear elsewhere.

GREEKING

Sometimes a language—when it dies?—
wants not to be spoken any longer, wants reality ousted
from every syllable and sign, free
to name its former life. Sometimes,
in the midst of each echo, it will
hearken back to cooing, or even farther,
to the blank page, and inter itself
in its luminous weight, a dying still
looking for a world to name.
       The alphabet is homo negro
and erases every trace of my name. I've borrowed
its debt—letters, glyphs, scrolls
against doors, biblical tablets,
daubed slate, chalk. Talking,
as we always talked, not about reason
with its speech bubbles: sentences
obscure to sense, death, pain. Steps that lead
nowhere except to airports
papered over with books about flight. Beyond water
with its blue-black punctuation beneath

fraying charts of light. Garvey said
the thread is stronger than iron. We said
nothing is sown. He said the secret sews
the possible. We said
the book remains untraced. Rabbi Jes said
the void makes him puke with boredom.
Everybody writes, taking the dialogues
to breathe more easily and enter the baths
with forgotten novels, discussing plot
and character, the never used pronouns, Ras's
invisible knights, and whether death exists
in each voice. We knew what this was—
a slashed name for weariness,
the concierge's posthumous annihilation, flesh
of the world. We sent our letters back to Jerusalem
and got back to work. And then, amid the pages,
syntax, weft, memes, no order or world. Suddenly the
illuminations burn, perish on the white page
with its pathos night after night.
Back then it was bizarre that,
after all that writing, we took sheaf from its trademark,
so inwardly gravitating to zero
beneath the stars. We were never lost.

Still later I think it makes sense that language should
lead back to death and silence
devote itself to the erased letters of the air,
a flight so inviolable it has little chance
of existing beyond the natural life of a poem.

COME THRU

I love
the weight
of unknown things

      the trace
           of a man's foot

which I watched, not
      for signs, but the nothing

that it leaves
beneath my feet, a sea

breaking into cloud
that has suddenly engulfed
          me,

pouring me to the core—
as if it illumined, not time,
nor the traces
      we leave,

but what vanishes
      in the downpour,

each word
      a threshold, a grindstone,
            a clay pit, a firing—

a thought
      that beggars
         reason
and what adheres to it:

a voice keyholed
        by what is found
but never owned,

by an eye
      that no sea
        can erase,

by wet sand
      crossed but untouched, crossed

              without space or volume,
or the imprecedent
        blush of erasure.

Who is it
that walks on the shingle shore
lost to all meaning,
who has disappeared
from the threshold
effaced from the world,
who enters the path
laid down
        like a fracture showering
                year, earth, mind, & word?

THE MONSTER

1

So take her there,
trembling, beside the Neversink,
beneath the swarm of midges,

the single garter muddied,
the voices—now naked—
fatal with consequence;

see her feelings darken
as the veil lifts
on the idol shielded

from the worst atrocities—
the red record so
blissfully intact

as her torment lingers
at the water's edge.
The white no sooner touched

than ready to go again,
with disgust and desire,
the body pressed to dreams of black.

2

So little the separation—
from red of sunset
to the whiteness of the moon:

the word ravished
spells death
as you run naked in the rain.

500 gather
in the narrow arteries
of Port Jervis;

manning the roads
far out
to the coutryside—

stiff with patience
till the sudden
bursting of the skies

rains down
upon them: the monster
in their midst

the last bloody act,
taught to learn slowly
each counsel of pain.

3

The trees cover over
the last remnants
of pollution:

the crowns green
the vented flesh
of rings bleached red

as leaves streaked
with the seeping,
the way desire falls,

or hatred is said to,
use every droplet
to cover the traces

of what was
wrought over in grief
on the boughs beneath.

He has closed my heart,
Lena said, his groans
black even in the act of love.

4

Then the storm broke.
And they said: this love was not love.

The object of his forceful suit,
not the woman lain down beside him

but all the stations of the morning,
choked by the dark now manifest.

To each neighbor
the plea of innocence

and wounds to leaven
an industry of blood.

THE DREAM OF MELBY DOTSON

Rocking—the train's motion—
that of an assault come alive,
in your throat,

the feet suddenly lifting
with a shudder
(your difficulty breathing)

to which cries
in the dark,
the fear is someone else's

(not yet yours), when
the only echo sounding
is that of your own crazed name.

Rocking,
and the fear of becoming—when, as now,
the chance of taking air

with a cricked neck surprises—
makes every dream a grave.
For the dream is inevitable

—and yes,
still with you
along with the thoughts that kill—

and spills from the closed lids.
This constriction
is not real;

but life in the eye of the dreamer;
for what he is
is only an echo to what he cannot know

is waiting;
(who urges him on)
himself dreaming in the realm of sleep.

THE DREAM, CALLED LUBEK

Now blacks, in the hold, working.
The harbors, overhung by mist. The canvas,
overseen by frost and rain.
The freest sea rides into port. The air
Refreshes ladies out on afternoon strolls, out for gain.

Perhaps the snow cleaves them,
their tongues passwords or gifts
concealed in dreams or memory
     of stars, else handed names
like coughs to sweeten the white acid-salt.
I am one of them like a glass in the sun.

As on a dark sea where no other is,
desolate in the screen never landing in desire;
wishes in with the tide, washed-up and tiered,
turning the sails onto dark horizons, onto dark rock;
seas of submergence
in which there is no place, no access,
cast out upon forgetfulness with no vessel,
pursued in the breakage of the wake.

To be myself inside the witness
where memory falls in remembrance
like a deluge; neither tribunal, nor excuses,
as I floated on the mirroring and a sail drew near,
nor withdrawal as the days and years become air and salt.

To be myself inside the witness,
witnessing the lost one never coming back,
all the recriminations and betrayals and disappointed lists,
as if in my thoughts there was a darkness,
without finitude or fascination,
which exists, has no burial, it resumes
neatly inside myself like an open grave.

To be adrift inside the reigning green,
deep in the midst and unfathomable seas,
overboard in the depths of each shining reflection
so false they return unnamed; a past never present,
down below a cloudless dark on the edges of waves.

On a road that is no road, the air dark with persistence:
the never-found names, appear. We receive
their iridescence in the form of human sewers and ashes.
We ensure their kenning through loss and sacrifice.

Knowing that the sacred cannot be housed here
after the silences of so many years,
        after the weaknesses of our disunity.
We return to what is lived in the barrenness
of what is desecrated, for tragedy is never enough
for what remains of us, nor what is lost the greener.

                    *

In the morning a heavy rain and wind came on.
Free as air
that scours from across the sea.
The last sheared tides as the lash speaks through
        what occurs, what cannot, what remains.

MURKING (AFTER STORMZY)

Think of a moment exploding
as a pulse
    leads us on
        into unaccustomed light—
   everyone astonished
     at the unerring cold
   of a thousand cellular voices.

The panic desensitized by suspicion.
The walls bathed in sweat.
Bodies in a heap forgotten in the basement.
Dis is no joke, star.
How many "yous knows-me?" are in this place?
Talk to anyone,
      violence is no more or less than beauty.

The sudden imploding trace,
   the realest codes
      flashing like sirens,
but there is no one here, so whose song is this,

still embracing still linking
   the downs that made us give up
 the towns that made shit one of the seasons
    the rain pouring
down all the elsewheres and maybe nevers
     of experience.

And here I am
   barefoot bleeding
  leaning against the po po
   so viciously off-key
from one imploding moment to the next
    (the human orphaned
      from its spirit),
where each thing granted is farther off (fenced)
    (and each random zero
   is beside itself with boredom)
     still murking
      still mired in the nevernever.

Me,
a man, singing in the circuits,
hearing

a voice bored by itself,
a voice reserved for nothing,
the smoked just too pure
for what really matters
when the fix remains too fixed
for the expanses   the distances
and passion is the least delirious
and what remains of the junk means
that what could not be made good
is the still point
of heaven.
(That's how it is—the infinite
always dissolving into leaven
like ash
in celestial fire,
the remainder
suddenly flooded with stars.) In me
a petrol-soaked carnage, its art
igniting fires on the streets.

JONAS RUNS THE VOODOO DOWN

1

The zombied dead forded:
the drawn integuments
ribbed, ash on the palings,
eyes unmoored from their shoring—

each verb a stone
to drop on the yellowed bones,
sunk in the ribs
the old language gutted.

Wind revives them,
sends them over low black hills
slow and soundless,
stumbling, ashen,

carried forth into the dark
only to expire
as day awakens—
the gods are sightless, he said.

The void that binds them:
pinholes, blood,
loa, painted wood:
a poet's childhood imaginings.

2

Turns out the light:
then he comes
like a quake inside you—
ossified by the cleaving

the body benched
as if by a drillhead,
each gasp possessed
in the cold and silence.

As he reaches in—muddied,
and finds your blackness
impenetrable, a tomb
to conjure in, a dam

to halt his dissembling,
a sootfall for each snow track—
you see an endless daylight,
gray, starless, bereft, a burned-up world.

The utter stranger is the poem:
like Lazarus exposed
but shorn of ground
unable to walk the distance.

HOERENJONGETJE

Pull down the ledger: it opens like a glib,
the leather sweat-soaked
in its clinkered cubicle.

Be sure that your fingers
do not smudge the rills and flanks—
sand should not be strewn on paper already dirtied.

The writ should not be black from the sentence.
Loose the flaps but not your tongue.
Release the words from their trap,

but don't forget to nuance the meaning.
This is where true ownership begins.
A hand scratching worth from zero.

THE REST UNFINISHED: IN DEDICATION
TO THE YOUNG NEGRESS, KARA E. WALKER

So strangely traced, as
a Rorschach test, Kara,
black skin stretched out upon wax,
wrested out of the tar
by the mouth of your sex,
from which the knife is mired
in a genteel history. White greasepaint
smeared in reverse,
to unmask the canebreaks,
except that it is not cork
that gets burned up,
but the ashen surface
of slavery. "A history that's still
living, very present," you say,
the silhouette cut, dark and black,
as you watch the ground it fills,
the ground loaded with cum
and cotton gins, in the swamps
bloodbaths from which the boy drinks,

as the white girl, dancing,
drinks headlong the wet shape of it,
her anus opened to plop things out
beneath the tall palladian window,
gaping like a beast
at the columned portico and the cock,
slave to the day's first light;
days and nights secured by
wire, by chains,
the white milk of daybreak
drank by massa in the darkened hall,
his lips clasped
on his light daughter's breasts:
as the tongue curves away to the south,
black shapes draped
on walls like feces,
slaves and masters hung
in the name of testimony—the gutted limbs,
malnourished babies,
and the serpentine trails
of blood and semen
fed in the name of darkened silhouettes
in which you stood, angry—

the paper stupefied
by the image, even though
cycloramas shake the wind;
longing to be free from the form
which held them,
where, in the fields, darkies
roll their eyes and moan amens;
outside the wind soughing,
as massa sits by the fire
stroking what even death can't undo,
where the sperm falls consecrated,
wedded to the tenderness of property
to which he is led by a slave's open mouth
that swallows all that he can give it,
until the tremor passes through him
and releases what he knows is his heart.

The paper drawn, cut:
"I wanted to create something
that looks like you...
it's a shadow, it's a piece of paper,
but it's out of scale." In your
tableaux of pain and perversity, Kara,

what swings into view
are slaves black against the darkness,
shivering, bunched, hideous,
their mouths open and empty,
yet full of transience and ash,
as they crawl towards the sedge,
skip and jump from the cabins,
in harness to the lifted skirts
of the confederacy. We need to look.
See your tableaux, their seminate legacy
heavy on the eyelid,
hauling wood across stubble fields,
soaking little missy in molasses
as she bathes
on a pedestal in the backroom,
her nest cut from the hearthrug, trimmed
by a young negress
dripping through house and driveway
as she hauls endless pails
of hot water
across mud and swampland,
smokehouses and patrollers,
across charred heaps of animals,

dripping water and milk, blood and shit
into the downspout of missy's mouth.
No way will the heroine return to us,
what she builds
is no longer carried by the ghetto
of her back—
let her cut out rings
in the back of her hands—there
beside the muddy road,
pushing out the world,
bloody, wrapped in rags,
that is surely not you, Kara.
As your glance steals us away
from the path of the big house,
your thirst for milk, for black milk
—the harvest bitter as sperm
white throughout the mouth—
the last of the passwords
voiceless by the roadside
as the horses and men passed.
You would tell Tilly
to cross the frozen river, not to look back,
cradling her belly in an image

of a moon already divided;
fragments of a world overturned
as she blinds herself on thorns
her body so lean it greedily
sucks dew and blueberries
from a dream in her head;
in her apron she carries her burned-up
heart, charred ever since childhood:
for what the eye reaches
reveals nothing but her disinterred grave—
falling open everywhere you look.
Let her grind and roll about in the ash.
The shadows cast by secrets—
what do they name, dogs and tracks,
out in the rain, legs open
with thoughts of what buds
on the breasts of desolation.
Let her climb up and suck
the air of the different
on her knees in the midst of freedom.
In her stomach big with nothing,
where language lies grave with life.

Today—it is the Endless Conundrum.
You feel it with your teeth,
you know it as tongue, as it zigzags
through the mantels, reflected darkly
as you stand unrecognized in the glass.
The banana skirt bears the look
of sacrifice—on your knees quivering,
as the piling-on of fetishes is, once again,
what makes possible whitenesses of image.
You feel something move in you,
your own thick-lipped litany
pouring out on the decks,
as the hunger of sailors
is made hot by dint of your dreamed-of hands—
the foetal dances
literally cut from your body, like paper,
scavenged from the wonderful warmth
of your veins—
the hottentot shape
long forgotten
because there is no other tale to tell.
Everything a stereotype.
Tell your skin—but how?

black as the all but black,
that there's an end to form
and its name is fate,
uncastable, unburiable, unmappable.
In the game of such terror, Kara:
the eye
that searches out, and spies, brings to light,
that fucks
in the long ago rememory of night;
the eye
that flees, and evades, and fools,
holding the void
that kindles you
together with you in the chasm,
as you speak
to the shared lineage and bloodlines,
drawn to what is there;
the eye
that reaches in through the meshes,
out towards the ploughed field, under
the glass of a collective frame,
thrust through the rim of meaning,
is death

in the shape of a woman, in the bed
of a bloodshrouded name.
If there is a gap. This is it.
The imagined,
suckled big with our black milk,
swollen like a creek, all the tributaries
incessant, held captive from mouth to slave,
weighed down, anchor-like
in the Tallahatchie river,
is something unaccountable—
a sword, a broom,
a row of urns, axes, and pumpkins,
and a runaway caught on the roadway.
They came upon him
carrying a razor and a severed hand.
They followed him,
followed and so went on
until they could see
the dull sulphur of his eyes—
a windowglass to migratory birds,
a mirror in which the mind veers,
never to be heard of again,
gone like mist from a river,
gone like the memory of a name.

NOTHING PRECIOUS IS SCORNED

1

December morning. It began with the cold pinch of winter, when the first chill fell on the clay of the cabins, and the thinnest shadows fell to earth as black ice swam across the eye of the lake and the dying sound of leaves fell into thoughts left frozen.

Perhaps it was the long pall that drew him, so early in the evening as he walked out into the chill air, perhaps it was the fast hardening ice thwarting his advance that spelled him as smoke tightened under foot and, cloudless, the night gave fullness to his waiting, watched by the animals as he mounted his horse. As he rides towards the cabins there is blood in his thoughts, a desperate wish to earn his spurs. The first time he raped her he said it was like banging his stick against multiple doors, or like pouring milk onto a black headstone. In any case, she was merely an ornament, a husk, an emptiness to be molded by force. Perhaps this is why he leaves her banged up and stammering into the night air, her mouth shattered, her body crushed and bleeding, her inner life become a thing of being. Perhaps this is why she weaves for him a dark cloth of bitterness where all that is torn trails mutely, a riddle that she trails from dusk to evening, a purl which she spins and unwinds with a voice no longer that of a girl. *The spun precarious weaves, secrets that she weaves for him alone.*

Days of oblivion, of uneasiness followed. Of separation, too. They looked at each other without a word. What could they say? They could only resist, only retreat into their difference. As a youth he had had nothing to lean against, nothing to rest on, he had felt orphaned in the fullest sense of the term, absent from himself, without weight, or reverberation, without hope. Now when he spoke it was with a master's voice, the semes landmarks of engendering. The keys lay in force. The morning after he tastes its privilege, and would swallow it if he could, but his vows mean that he doesn't have to. This only compounds the cruelty. After such bitterness, is it any wonder she should seek to reenter the warm baths of nonexistence? Imagine nothing and in the middle of nothing a brief shadow. What if you were told this tiny opacity is you? Without rights and protections, without childhood, without past, chained to the absence of being, your being a stone. No one can lose more than the slave loses; it is a loss molded by violence as the inner life drains away. But what is force? It is an act in which all are implicated, but the force of that "all," as of the implication, remains uncertain. And not everyone is equal to its weight.

2

With these black threads that pass through her fingers she unravels the world. With each spool she unwinds all that she has ever been and all that she was allowed to be. She spins loss after loss. Seated in darkness, turned away from the night whose stars mirror the work of her hands, she sews unseeingly, weaves the cloth with bright red threads. Her tireless fingers shuttle between the lace-bands and bone. A scream goes through her as she severs the threads. She pierces the night with her needle, but her blood merely pricks the web of shame. Humming a song that only she knows, she wonders about this rage sewn into her, this weft that makes the scissors blunt as stones.

Seated in darkness, spinning loss after loss as night doubles her stitches, she weaves without end, spins threads dark as clouds.

With no fire in the cabin the day soon became night as the wind banged on the shutters and the rain, furious, lingered in pools before entering the room. She sat waiting, in her shrewd eyes was a sort of refusal, a revolt, and on her milky forehead appeared a sort of venomous calm as she watched sloping shadows fall on the moon soaked pallet which, for years, had forbidden any message except the tale of her defeat. Outside, the dogs sat quivering as night entered the dark fields. Finally she hears him calling out, in fervent braids, the collar of her name, walking across the flooded fields on his way to the cabins. When he enters she flushes crimson and, for a moment, she is hesitant, subdued; in her own way her desires have gone elsewhere, beyond imagining—at the sight of him she finds herself dazzled; the world was white and it had already pierced her, lifting her skirts, branding her profane. But as he steps over the threshold, wearing a look smudged with courtesy, wet and heavy with charm, something tumbled inside of her and she heard her heart collapse... The first blow bloodied his head and eyelid, the second blow forced him to hang his neck down, the third dispossessed him of his strength forcing him to slump onto the pile of skirts, silks, and stockings, his eyes wide and doleful in the lace-work, his mouth opening and closing like a fish caught in a net.

On each intricately knotted thread the image of all that she had lost: and, in the silence disturbed by him, a long lingering word whispered again and again—coming, as it were, after the rain and ashes—a rutting word for the years she lay naked, pinned beneath him, lashed to the spools, weaving a thread of mockery for that which no longer covered him, the force that saw in her the purest of mirrors.

But two questions remain. Did he know, when his conquering hands lifted the veil, what he would discover in her eyes, hanging there by a long black thread? Did her weakness later seem a lesson to her masters, and to him, an essential test leading to their particular consciousness of existence, to the acceptance of a life lived along the slay?

THE "SECRET" OF THIS FORM ITSELF

it begins at the border
                intimate as skin
searching for a sentimental foreignness or fusion
        all these restless voices
reflected in the antiplace
        where we enjoy the status of victims
the disease and compensation
        tricks of fate?

when we stepped off the boat
        the tide, the long imperial gain,
extended to all colonies,
debased by the raw stink,
the world retched in the advocacy, we were the script—

what secret
        emerges from these idylls of nations,
                at the mercy of ringworm gods
                        arteries open
                wide to the

                                        purity of island stories—
do we love the obsession,
        this way of being a blocked wall
screening out more desolate places?

as when wading through a warm stinking mess
                            to meet my father,
lightscreens in the back of my cropped skull,
a whirlpool of shapeless heads screaming in the darkness
        I want to let go—but cannot
there is no consolation, the opaque derision
anonymous, racially compelled

I didn't know air could burst into white flame
                or that the weak,
dying on an outlying island,
        could sing useless lieder of queens and empire

I would love to lock the door
        ease the flood
fresh on last night's storm
safe,
this landed world a dream
edifice of scaffolds

what emerges is an unmistakable symmetry
      driving their buses
      their trains, wiping away
all the blood and foulness of their arses,
making tea with sugar seeing
      the chains and mutilations
      done by cultured men
framed for posterity
          on the horizon of an idea

pressing their way
into the long sweet paralysis
of so many years lost, wandering
      adrift in memory

this space that is open to us could so easily be lost
      we have neither the books nor the city
only the many reflections of polished floors and corridors
      a surfeit of forgotten traces without rank or honor

I didn't know the depths of these unspoken things,
         or why I had to wait until 1963
to sound them out in the parade of a new age

watching adidas shop-windows and gold chains
                    the repeated denials
along the way drifting back to the real.

MOVEMENTS, MONUMENTS

Negerisch wohnet der Mensch

1.

The greatest threat is from blackening clouds,
which is why possibilities emerge
with the sound of birds, and voicelessly
fly back to destruction; day dark rounds
like promises made at a fork in the road—
this is how things come, and go,
become a parting of the ways,

a fall infinitely gentle, unfortunate.
Of which it is said
force, like lightning,
is penned in by distance.
And yet I haven't been breathing now for seventy years.
I think it's because I'm sick, or stupid.
Skinny with sickle cell, fat with uneasiness.
The coming storm will not save me.

A vast sea of *vogelfrei*
who neither go back nor disperse,
and who, "untamable," are hurled down,
defaced, are my sweetest obscenity.

As if the breathed in air was evening,
a golden mask to gag on.
It takes plenty of cunning not to
confound freedom with contagion, compliance with will.
Soon we'll be living like ghosts
passing through menacing doors,
gazing upon the nakedness of our lives
like the last, excluded customer,
for this here's not the place for you—
locked down in pronoun,
resigned to everything simile.

2.

And in the morning
I am finally able to join the long queues of funerals.
The line is slow and strangely noisy
before the creators call it a night and go home.

The rooms we live in
cloistered in silence and unforgettable elements.
In every corner there is scarcely believable dust,
and metaphysical holes full of human ambiguity.
Everything closer is far away,
and everything certain never was.

It's been awhile
since the rope and the hemp
were so stoically, lovingly held
by those held down to slaughter.
And it does seem that a crack
has appeared in every thing witnessed.
I am thinking of a crown,
a surplice, a blackly domed landscape.
Life leads us out of it, time closes us in.
But time itself gives us pause.
And each marbled suspense
is itself suspended with pinpointed strokes,
and every terrible moment
equal to a slaughterhouse (a life bloodied).

Sister, sometimes I feel
gaslit by the postman,

as if the unknown is my address
and "no one at home" the sender.
Everything lived for someone else's proof of purchase.
The unsigned check the closest thing
to redemption
(despite the strange shame in cutting it).

3.

You've seen all this before:
the unkind kindnesses, the unremarked surrender—
when the only lives lost are routinely black,
and it dawns on you
that the only one to lie
is the one flush with deception,
whose illusion is taken on trust
because it is the source of all sickly resolution;
the scams by which we are caught on insta,
when the price of a platform
is the freedom to hand over one's identity
willingly, like a boyhood faith in invulnerable gods,
where everything seems possible—
the nothingness of a desire unable not to desire.

Who can say give it back
when to be stolen is just
the stuff of dreams, one's identity
nothing more than a sheet of paper
on which is written, not truth,
but an endless self-portrayal
of an unknown purpose or nature?
As if the ink were a mirror,
                    a medium,
and each word a lifestyle guru,
a maze shaped into image, franked & stamped
by an unreachable hopefulness?

Stay disappeared, says milk:
                    naked as the day
that once more crowns you
a victim of everything you are,
blindsided, duct taped,
        superglued to each purple tweet,
and each composed selection
haloed, bloodshot,
by lonely unspent misery;
and in return

our blind hands
perform yet another version of persuasion,
mirroring the algorithmic immensities
of what we virtuously imagine to be
what we know and know not to be
virtuous, or true.

4.

"As any child will tell you,
perhaps we are too rarefied
to link up, too extra
not to throw shade."
Your words sharper than pepper spray
before the air desecrates us. Until today

to be an other
was to be true to an insatiable wish
to please, but no longer.
There's no more whiteness—just the wish
to break out of our improper dark;
no time to bode
the stranger who breathes beside you,

the grey hordes waiting at the caring gate.
But who can return us back to ourselves,
when distance is neither place nor departure,
and being-with is nothing but horror,
a crater in each solitary terrain,
the force detonating—by reinforcing—distance?

5.

It's probably why
others plummet on waxen wings,
or loom up from innumerable seas,
on beaches where promises are bait rings
and what surrounds us is something shocking, colossal,

without amnesty,
heavy with astonishment & pulled teeth.
This absurdity in which cruelty is *de rigeur*,
cloud-burred and so much more than virtue?
Yes, you who walk without right or conscience?

For loneliness is the manure
from which each thought blooms,

and anxiety is just a rug to be beaten,
a dog lovingly walked to death
in wheatfields camouflaged by machinery.

Like almonds milked white by being crushed
and swallowed in one gasp
so as to be kept secret,
each step follows innocence
and every breath opens its mouth to destiny.

6.

A page turns, and each word burns.
Curfews ebb like suns
of reined-in disappointments, black lives
like leaves the nighttime sheds
like week-old lottery tickets.
The river you step in. And for the innocent,
a vast swarm of birds.
Nothing—can you feel it?—
a kind of jam for tough eggs,
and every loving hope wished-for
shadow upon shadow of seething doubt—

the way a marbled depth
black with cloud
plummets in confederacy.
For passion needs no other,
it holds nothing but itself.
The looking-glass a shard of so much cynicism.
A stumbling block, an empty pail of water.
The awaited, changeless, epiphany
of crushed mouths under black stars.
Bulbs flicker under huge trees, and, what is more,
manifest a world of number and simile.
A light only half discernable, barely believable,
black as birds set free.

FALLEN, RISING, A SACK FULL OF SYMBOLS

All night the rain
persistent, in
swells and puddles, our rival.

Beneath the dark water
a deeper water is rising,
absorbed in the work of creation.

A misshapen, formless thing,
not yet earth or air,
hauls itself forward

lurching under the branches
into thickets
of deception, each step a churning mud—

and very slowly,
like a mountain shaking free the earth,
it emerges warm and moist into the wetlands.

What am I
but a dark storm rising
above the wet black earth

a bad smell
full of fear and desolation,
thick and dense as a sewer airing its abandoning.

What am I
but these fords of discontent
so insistently wetted, the cool air

never the release
(from discord bridling)
but the reminder, of rain, its hardnesses on lakes
                                        and mountains.

Gore-washed and heavy
I rain down the great doors. I enter the silence of the hall.
Each motionless form so easily reddened,

grabbed and folded, bent and torn.
They weigh almost nothing in my hands
as they yield to the changes

I pull out of them,
their open mouths
devastated by the sluicing recalibration.

Mother, a storm is in the air,
you don't need it
to become a river, or to flood

these otherwise dry
borders, to become
a new ark for our damned world.

Something still glistens,
and is falling (between us)
somewhere between sky and earth.

BEFORE WHITENESS

The whiteness of things comes out late
—ANDRÉ DU BOUCHET

1

"This text is a ring.
A cocked ding-a-ling.

I know this
sounds a bit silly,

but there is a ferocity
here,

and for that reason,
a language that precedes language;

it came on the trains,
and I can't help feeling,

it gets lonely,
which is why

it wants to strike you:

I know it sounds strange,
that I decided
to go back on the trains,

and that I
ended up in Ledbury,

and was struck
repeatedly, atrociously,

until my sex parts were gone
and my face past hoping,

but I wanted
to pay a visit
to my grace,

and I didn't have a car,

and I didn't have enough
money

for a taxi.

2

"So I had a cup of tea,
and I said to mama:

the place we live in
is not nice and not safe;

on the streets
there is nothing but glass, junk, and blood.

People speak to you
in incomprehensible languages,

as if they were
conspiring in a rain of ashes,

or leaning out of shattered minds.
And our neighbors

are the most horrible fucking monsters
I've ever seen.

It's a world away
from paradise, a city in name alone.

But there is no risk until evening breaks forth.
No triumph that is not darkly illumined.

3

"Everything began with the influx,
the black fluencies, before the war.

The fear
that pursued me to the docks;

the chasms
that told me I was a marked man;

and the dark hours
where a city within a city beckoned

but I could not enter
because I was the furthest one behind,
and I had precious little idea of where I was.

These things exist, and, what is more,
they have a system,
but none that could protect me, and none that made sense.

4

When mama and I are alone
(neither I nor Thou),
she tells me not to think anything of it,
just to wade in and take my chances.

And I thought I am a good citizen,
even though I have been revisited
by so many catastrophes and ill beginnings.

And so the years went by.
I wanted to leave our stone tower,
but the pressure gave me migraines,

and that's when everything went to hell.

5

I went down to the city
because I had to get away from mama,

and because I wanted to see my grace.
I was like a bride
waiting for time to stop, but when it did

I grew fearful, and I wanted to turn back,
but every door led to anguish, dark disappearing paths,

and every circumstance
to accursed innocence, for all was evil. How often,

bludgeoned into oblivion,
was I told I still have the look of paradise?

Yet I can't even get out of my bed,
let alone clean myself.
I lie for the sake of lying and will shag anybody.

And I felt glad
that I didn't care and was condemned.

As I walked past burning cars, looters on skateboards,

and I spoke to prostitutes leaning up
against noticeboards,
and I said: fucking hell what's that smell?

And a man sleeping in a cot said, give us a kiss, luv,
and I thought whoooo!
Since when has living been easy money,

where everything is permitted us
and we get to
wear contempt like an ill-fitting costume
and aren't even capable of doing a thing?

6

*"Then the next thing they kicked the door open
and about eight of them came in."*

O spirit! the intellectual power
of poets without repose,
and who come at the end
of so many artifices and dangers,

and whose worship
is the equal of any artistry;
and before whose indescribable, sublime magnitudes
we are found wanting:

I have walked among them
dirty, unclean,
and in desolate isolation:
shall I then say that they made me sick,

and forced me
to lie in puddles of vomit, and once held
that being held was a force of law,
and to be spat on was a dream made to fit the ledger. . . ?

7

I am climbing
God knows where.

I can hear
the mockery of sailors,

the way they scale
the taut veil of the air,

and hone
the obscure weight,

the indescribable lightness of day,
the sails suspended

like a drug that makes no difference
to my bruised, embarrassed body.

A light
strikes the rigging of my eye,

as if day itself
had mocked its own obliquity,

or the *sun* had deepened
into something wordless, beyond all thought—
and I had time enough
to listen, or to hear,

and the world didn't sound so unhappy
like an orphan (swollen, malnourished),

shivering in the corners of these cells.

8

"This text is a ring. A tin full of pins.
In it mama stumbles on the mat,
before moving out
(she's wearing all black):

the foul smell
of reefer swarms all over
the building, like a deal
gone wrong:

it stalks her to the last end
of the flowering earth.
Her breath falls like crystal fire.
She is furious, without reprieve,

and yet we turn to look at each other.

It's the end of the journey.
The tower collapses like rubble, a mountain blown apart.
Ink moves over the paper like floodwater over a dark field.

9

"This text is a ring.
A pong inside a ping.

What a little bleeder you are,
the first translator says,
wailing about a little coke,
as if it voids all life and vigor,
harboring only fear, disquiet?

And you, faith, if only you were
here, if only you could see who
is undressing me on the couch.

Thus do I reach down,
witness to the long, impractical excavations,
my mercury entranced by crystal breaths.

Let's finish the bottle, first,
before I wreck myself on you
my hull sunken in the ice
enrapt by your lightless depths.

And when all was done, and finished,
the beloved's
disillusions shone like stars in darkness.
But without mama I couldn't imagine hope, snow or grace.

10

I wanted to go see mama,
but my fingernails ached,
and my faith felt crippled, not by love,
but by the lost sureties of being a pirate

needing to live in enchanted lands,
eyeing my terrain
beneath bridges with ogres
who frightened me, terrified me,

who were to content to chase me
to the dynamited houses, but no further.
As for being a pirate,
what good was my perfected appearance,

my camouflaged image
in the water, if I hurt all over,
and all the ogres I loved
took away my lunch money and shoes

leaving me to clear away
all the knives and plates from the table?

11

And I thought, little Prince, how I pity thee,
standing alone at the bar,
with neither friend nor enemy,
hurling arterial plumes in the corridor.

Have you ever had a home?
It seems that uncertainty was your father,
whose frozen air clouds your face
and makes you seem older than you really are.

Just remember to sing the plainest things,
the vast soul-like sounds of what is,
the sound of two girls uncrossing their legs,

and at the summit you'll answer the furious summons
of God (his eyes perfunctory and debilitated),
but you will go on singing
into the mustachioed depths of cloud.

For the world has never loved you
and will not pay the bill for you,
and will not surrender its sullen, parenthetical burdens.

12

"This text is a ring.
It is dense
as a doting fool: a world with its flies open.

I used to visit the girls at Riverside.
I'd park up and walk through the burnt-out slums
at night mostly,
on the trail of sweet little pouts,

melodious angers, bodies without sex.
I know it sounds strange
but I liked talking to the girls:
it felt like I was awakening, that I was imagined.

But it was dark and no one saw me or recognized me,
and even I looked surprised
when she said
she'd been waiting for me,

with my sad, baggy breeches
and my cutlass always slipping down,
and my eye patch
winking transcendentally at the bluing void.

Then my mind started screaming,
and my arms and legs
became pinnacles and mountains,
and I felt like I was at a cliff edge.

I saw she was angry and upset
for the way she spoke
was graced by a new kind of irritation.
How could she say those things?

Why couldn't she see what I felt like...
The prodigious luminosity of all that surging water,
the many vigils held
on the blackest heights...

And I was outside my number,
awed by the threshold
of time slowing, glassy blood in the vein.

I think of all this at the sea,
the source of so much misunderstanding,
as I bathe my feet
in its deep phantom beauty,
the water more swiftly flowing
where what is heard
is saturated by water;
and perhaps I catch a glimpse
of caverns empty but echoing
at the edge of the sea.

It is a sound that no sound can pierce—
(I can see my blood flow, like a gas,
as atoms cleave and stun the heart
in its infrequent motion.)

That's when she asks me to leave.
And I tell her
the universe, too, is growing cold;
look at how
it burns in separation, in imbalance,
and at the same time
casts unceasing shadows upon the veil;
the deep, unfurling waves
that leave us stranded here,
as the sea itself disappears
like fading newsprint in the hallway,
and all the traces incomplete, desolate.

13

That was how the little Prince spoke
in vague hints, but with the most earnest of vows
pure in his nakedness,
his voice sad and lifeless.
And what of the glaciers, the black rain of birds
in the whitest of snows?
The unfamiliar slopes we walked on, with cold hands?

Didn't you once, Mama,
hidden behind these dreamless, black draperies,
once say that death and birth are,
to the adverting mind,
like wilted trees
with no leaves left on them?
You, too, dislike the wilderness;
the impious noisiness of Crichton Street;
the office blocks and factories,
in which the living have neither use nor sense,
and where weeks of loneliness are resolved
                                    through masturbation.

Come here, to the unknown
version of this room
where all power is, and all names,
and, lying on the slopes
of so many decisions and hesitations,
my voice slowly receding
in the reflected chasms of your silence,
O my Mama, I will want all from you,
all fears, disguises, and disagreements;
I'll silently study your face…

the voiceless, inaudible singularity
of your thoughts wandering in darkness
(These atoms are tumultuous, diverse,
infinite, and deeply frozen in utter vacancy!)

14

"This text is a ring.
It will see justice done; a poor devil caught bang to rights:

a single man
who lives with his mama.

Who writes as one
returning to the scene of a crime.

With tips
of wrought iron, pegged in brass,

the glint
of scythes in dark December woods:

animals, chattels,
variously sounded in dirt and saliva,

a pitch or intonation
languidly fallen or dead,
a shout that is precipitated

before its meaning is pronounced
in the darkness, without coherency,

like a face repeatedly punched,
the hands handcuffed,
punched, kicked, then punched again

until every word is believed,
and every pause fateful,

the inability to speak signifying, at such moments,
the sound of being assaulted,

or taking the piss, as if one had smiled and pleaded
for another sentence, or even

pursued an artifice of dust—a fall, then,
Throw him through the fucking window,

when what keeps happening
is the point at which one surrenders,

and
You're dead whatever happens,

the punch in the mouth
like the final stroke of a pen,

the flawed urgency
of a different expectation;

the violence heard in other rooms
mere background noise

that remains unknown, invisible,
an infinity of zeros:

gens sans feu et sans aveu,
and the sense there
that what is henceforth heard
has no reprieve or identity,

that the mark will remain
after speech, the incrimination

foreshadowed in the pleasures
of articulation—the mask of spirit

absolute, unreadable, unbroken.

15

"gens sans feu et sans aveu:
whatever this speaking is
it will be held
down, harassed, attacked, for all eternity.

Wordless, collapsed, rapped for illegal pilfering,
the shouts of the oppressed
a moment in history,
the blows by which all secrecy is known,

and turned into something inexplicable, uncertain;
the inchoate groans
meeting the ferocity of a refused hope,

the hard sound of truth and glory

(wiped like blood from the lips)

the wounds yellowed, in shadow;
the child's disappearances barely seen in frozen mists.

Coda

Through crowded trains
in which I cry and am
but an isolated fury,

listening
to several voices,
as day comes up out of dirtied windows,

I write of this shame
so as to possess it,
and to idolize its pride, its black nobility.

GOODBYE PORK PIE HAT

because it is
hidden,
secret (*geheim*),
    & all traces
of it
  impenetrable,
  distant,
like sirens
  blissfully
    sounding in the dark,
what enters
  so assiduously
    broken
is also
  what ends—the enforced meaning
(*Stop! Police!*—how it enters the fray)
  after all
    no one really knows
      what words want
        (these songs wearing peasant shoes

on strange stumpy legs)
the scattering
random, bloodstained
& everyone running in the streets

as someone
hears it
once again
(the unluckiest brightlit arrangements
of burnt ships fired into flame!)
as it enters
the bones
like a harmony
that awaits
you
& everything
just chokes
the world
assiduously
gasping for
air
amid the noise
of infantries

                         (clouding
                                  all sense),
          the unbridled rush
                  to find them
                                  —like barricades unveiled—
              on video
                  after the briefest
                          command—*Run*—
          is impeded
            by the wild,
                  intemperate
            meandering
                  of silence and sex
            & the big foaming
                  mouth
            announces that every rib
                  is cracked
                                  again

                  by the *haute volée*
                                  of each utterance
              when being
                  human

involves just listening

to the rain (the revenge of elegies),

& mastery is just

the impermanent, briefest

of rests

in desperate resorts

where we know it all ends

& I am you

& each wishful

moment

is a decapitation,

a thought

that twists

because what it notices

it no longer lives,

& it is impossible

to say

no, too soon

& how

suddenly

(the sea burns,

drowned

parched by flame), & someone beckons

& reminds you
     that each gathering
          is a celebration
          of the already dead
and
  each word
    matters
less than
  it should,
     (the hard facts
          fluttering
               like banners
                    over bloodsoaked pavements)

& methinks
     there are years
          here
ranged like so many antlers,
  memories
     of cognac & latin,
as anarchists

start slashing
at pictures once again
& you cut *here* and *here*
the asymptotic glimpses
of dark fluent sequels
in Berlin, London,
& the great gates
of Ishtar
where all the shrouds
are veiled—
which can only mean
that life is a *Fälle* (a theatre)
or that someone
(the wealthiest art lover)
has reached
down
into each word
and cut out
the name of each cameo
or is it simply
because I miss you
running
through the rain-drizzled streets

and all I have

are

(clouds

rioting

in dark, ancestral languages)

I.M. SEAN BONNEY

CLASH CITY POETS

Yes, grey skies, when the typewriter can only write failure
and the high syllables hiss like rain in
the traps, the indifferences, or sorrows, virtual
and not the pages on the table before us,
the catastrophe endless as the sea. Yes,

the smell of rain in the air,
as water makes the world legible
before the damp wood in a heap at the door
reminds us
of the first moments forever sought, forever lost
the rise and fall
asking to be marked
like the slit ears of a slave.

That part about a choice we can believe in
dying for inertia, when pleasure or arousal
has no scale, like traffic
when every direction is undeserving,
and what will not change is change itself,
wading through the rivers

to the scented reed banks
as rain ponders me like a sister, reckless blood.

How imprisoned we are, how fastened
everywhere scanned
through apertures,
waiting days to sleep
without the means to step into the world
without the strength to escape it
without anything but
a peephole into who we are.

Here, with notebooks in hand,
the rain greets us the way people used to do.
The smell of it receding
on the headland, thick with burnt limbs.
A mishap rejoined to a serviceable truth.

In cinders, also,
as the city covers our footprints,
and we reach the other shore,
soon, the feeling that *beauty*
is never as beautiful as we are now.

That it should have been you, beside me,
and not the ones who betrayed her, the CEO
who stonewalled every question we asked,
the poets who quarrel no more,
the bridesmaids
who sailed into the black sleep of never land
and listed all the sins,
bringing us down to earth.

I.M. DAMBUDZO MARECHERA

LESTER YOUNG BY WASHINGTON SQUARE

Some day I shall catch my breath
alone in a dark room with the sky clear, clear.

I shall listen to the radio playing
Pennies from Heaven in the filthy air.

The sky will be washed clean of birds
and a dog will bark just once

amid this song of yearning
as I pass from the world

in my mouth this curious taste.
I shall whisper a word I don't know,

a word that means nothing to me
as it passes from me into the bright world.

A world of desolation as I lie choking
on the damp bed while all the years

enter the history of sleep
and never to come again

except as footnotes to this music
rising in the air.

Loneliness, disaster, gall.
I shall hoard each in this room.

Pay a price I cannot name, and lose all
as light fades on my broken body.

The sudden flight of birds
will leave the sky clear

as they pass from sight, while music rises
on dreams laden with longing

breathless in my ear.

BLUE IN BANDOE

Say true to yourself:
take a draw, but don't speak,

the eye bloodied
by feeling, heartbreak;

and a mouth that says
it is time to talk about what cannot be seen,

that weighs
so delicately the fatigue of bone

behind plaster walls
humming—

where the dream
is simply the air breathed in, the wounds,

firm as the chance
that went missing, honeyed in ruins:

and all faces, all escapes,
ecstatic with the heightened manifestation

that God himself
brings closer with each convulsion!

A body owned, scarred,
but grown old in the newlyweds' bed;

the aspirated fall of deep sadness
like a bridal witness

who has forgotten the ring,
the party long since departed—

and how helplessly splayed
everything is, your exhausted rush

to be ceasing and, as it were,
ceaselessly wanting

nothing but this:
orgies of sound

less pleasure, a pleasure
sweeter for being filled

by the delirious, tedious approximation
of water in a desert, blood in the till.

I.M. BOB KAUFMAN, 1925–1986

ANOTHER BURNING

this paper is on fire

                        being
human, as it incinerates itself
lit from within—
as if being of earth
was itself to be earthed,
a shock: a final, purifying stroke,
lighting up
        the most dangerous approach.
                        descending.

this paper is on fire
and the earth is a room
inside the flames
            incinerare
                    breathed
            like a rope of air

where we took
our final, faltering steps
down smoke-filled stairs,
down narrow corridors
a roaring in our ears
openmouthed, blindsided,
our throats already burning
from the portrayal.

And I
like you

among the mute, the breathless,   *g*
the thrice-taken denials
never promise enough.
every stumbling step
a forest you struggle through,   *r*
waiting, penned in—
can't you hear it
approaching ....   ,
the crumbling columns of desuetude   *e*
the summits heaving, sweating

out surprising wisps of air?

like an exhalation rushing over rags,   *n*
you, roadmen, doused & sussed,
uttering the tolls
for the longest journey.   *f*

like a word
falling easily through inflamed lips—   *e*

blackness
wasn't in the language—we saw it   *l*
being evacuated
but we still inhabited
            the ashes.   *l*

the obscure, obsolescent
        threshold
                never entered,
already neglected,
        never spotted, never grasped.

the *impasse*—unable to go up or down
in the prosaic light of faith, tiptoeing
to catastrophe.

words
    falling
        ever
            downwards   (the air on fire)
(and as we stumble forward,
a vacuum:
                we breathed in its ferocity)
to fall, like
a word,
a word not yet
fallen, but burning,
separated,
unable to cross from landing to safety—
a fall
that has not yet happened:
                the breath
                that you don't own
                is not yours
                to breathe—

hear them: the long doomed
iftar, the already ashen bolari,
and, in the black smoke,
a discarded *belgha* left
lying in the ruins—

each sentence meaningless
          as tall burning buildings loom—
          and time ceases,
          staggered by fear & shame—
          a storey in each story
          (each falling). the
          story is the storey
          within the building
          built on charred names.

at the end of the
          day, dust
settling, breathed in,
as each gaze turns away,
          and there's nothing
to distinguish a tower from an incinerated outline.

This paper is on fire
     lifted out into
        the void
   into lives lived without air.
             the unknown heights

recognized   in rooms where there is no
              emergency exit.

there is no trace,   for here,
everything is lost
    trapped without rescue:
      and each room
         is a cliff   where we are
           perched on
       a rim of burning flame,
     and each door
         is a vista   where we shall
       be shipped back to the blaze
  brought back to the unknown
    shore
      like birds
         returning back

                    to unachieved seas,

                                    the untold *dis*
                        of our dear fallen

                                    heirs
                    transported from earth into air.

            and the fire breaking in
            waves—a sea from which we were never
            meant to be rescued, or leave: every sentence, then,
            a station of the last: the buckle
            that stays because it can't be grasped—

    still, the tower stood there, still, beyond mere sorrow,
    beyond what may be told and what may not,
    beyond the burning calms, and each soul a window
    illumined by their petrifying ripostes:
    and every breathed-out word reflected
    on the melting surfaces, the spines of what
    will survive us: both scaffold and shipwreck—
    as the more dangerous storeys become air and violet
    moths, and each spark an oblivious brute annulment
    of the white glare of departure.

whiteness
the height that rains

and sets to right the rightless
ingloried
leaven
as we flame out,
        burnt to a crisp—

incinerare—

    the whiteness of place unplaced
    beyond
    language, the last refuge
    of loss—
    and the unburned
    waiting awaited
    word
    cast out without hope
    or arrival.

    this paper is on fire

where even names go missing,
and the earth's lapsed, burnt-out
symbol is a medium, a building,
its cladding explodes *here*
over tumbling heaven-drenched air:

this paper burns itself,　　　　it ascends
　　　　over the word's
　　　　　　　　black shadowless stains—
and what it unveils it eradicates.
the lives lifelessly resident in unlived places
where no one wants to live, towering
　　　　over what ceases
in the flames,
　　　　　　　　the charred remains
rising beyond thresholds
　　　　of belonging, unliving.

　　　　　　incinerare—

　　　　it rapidly crosses the open
　　　　the remains inside the ear
　　　　that crosses what passes on—

blackness sifted, blanched,
let go, dumped, left in dismay.

g   *r*   *l*
    e
n   *e*
   f   *l*

              this paper is on fire

it cannot breathe
    it will crumble
        into dust
like a building
    that forms itself
        into a word
    the tap tapping of an
ashen wing
    that frees itself
        from everything that is air,
   O my unhoused Chevalier!
become a weightless slave

that no room confines
　　　　and no refuge,
　　as if fire were speaking itself:
the word *due*
　　　　expectant but so ruinously
　　　　　　unplanned,
a kind of death-trap
　　　　for
　　　　　　the word *owing*—
　　　to grasp in order to never be grasped
　　　by the ungrasped *always*,
　　　　　　suspended, freed,
from descent as well as any rescue
　　　　　　　　　　lived for,
　　　the paper, unwilling.

　　　　　　　　　　　　for you and I
descent meant rescue,
　　　　　　　but there was black smoke
all around us,
　　　　　and our mistake was in thinking
that language meant

> expectancy or survival—
and not something endlessly abandoned,
> > > evacuated.
a word petrified, then cracked.
> > a void endlessly imprinted,
> > > shaped into concrete.

NOTES AND ACKNOWLEDGMENTS

"The Ghost of Averages"
"French grammar": A reference to Booker T. Washington's *Up from Slavery* (1901).

"Lorem Ipsum"
"funny peasant shoes": A reference to Martin Heidegger, "The Origin of the Work of Art," in *Poetry, Language, Thought* (1971).

"Black Sunlight" was published in *The Penguin Book of the Prose Poem: From Baudelaire to Anne Carson* (2020).

"little aspen tree": A reference to John Ruskin's chapter, "Fontainbleau," in *Praeterita* (*Works*, Vol. XXXV).

"Come Thru"
The poem includes reference to Daniel Defoe's *Robinson Crusoe* (1719).

"The Monster"
This poem includes reference to Stephen Crane's novella, *The Monster*, and the Port Jervis lynching on which it is based.

"The Dream of Melby Dotson"
This poem refers to a bizarre 19th century lynching that was the outcome of a lynching dreamed. Having fallen asleep on a train, Dotson, when wakened from the nightmarish dream of his own lynching by a white conductor, believed he was being actually attacked and so assaulted the conductor. An act which led to him being lynched. For details see William Ivy Hair, *Carnival of Fury: Robert Charles and the New Orleans Race Riot of 1900* (1976).

"The Dream, Called Lubek"
The title references "The Jesus of Lubek," one of the first slave ships, and the artwork "A Ship Called Jesus" (1991) by Keith Piper.

"Jonas Runs the Voodoo Down"
The title is a pun on a track from Miles Davis's 1970 album, *Bitches Brew*. The Jonas referred to is the Boston poet, Stephen Jonas, who died in 1970, and who wrote *Exercises for Ear*.

"The Rest Unfinished"
Citations are taken from MoMA Online Projects, "Conversations with Contemporary Artists," transcript of a conversation with Kara Walker, 1999, http://www.moma.org/onlineprojects/conversations/kw_f.html; and Jerry Saltz, "Kara Walker: Ill-Will and Desire," *Flash Art 29*, no.191 (November/December, 1996): 82–86.

"Nothing Precious Is Scorned"
The title is taken from Simone Weil, "*The Iliad*, or, The Poem of Force."

"The 'Secret' of This Form Itself"
Title taken from Karl Marx, *Das Kapital*, Volume 1.

"Movements, Monuments"
The epigraph is a pun on the famous line by Friedrich Hölderlin, "dicterish wohnet der Mensch" from the poem, "In lovely blueness." "*vogelfrie*": meaning "free as a bird, not bound," but also to the state of being banned. See Karl Marx, *Das Kapital*, Volume 1.

"Fallen, Rising, a Sack Full of Symbols"
This poem alludes to the Old English epic, *Beowulf*.

"Before Whiteness"
This poem includes reference to André Du Bouchet's poem, "From the Edge of the Scythe"; Antoine de Saint-Exupéry's *The Little Prince*; and Martin Buber's *I and Thou*. The phrase, "gens sans feu et sans aveu," is taken from French Medieval law.

"Goodbye Pork Pie Hat"
The title is taken from Charles Mingus' 1959 composition for Lester Young, which appeared on the album, *Mingus Ah Um*.

"Clash City Poets"
The title is a pun on the 1978 song, "Clash City Rockers," by the Clash.

"Another Burning"
The poem is a response to the Grenfell Tower fire in June 2017. It includes a reference to Gerard Manley Hopkins' "The Windhover."

The state of the world calls out for poetry
to save it. LAWRENCE FERLINGHETTI

CITY LIGHTS SPOTLIGHT SHINES A LIGHT ON THE WEALTH
OF INNOVATIVE AMERICAN POETRY BEING WRITTEN TODAY.
WE PUBLISH ACCOMPLISHED FIGURES KNOWN IN THE
POETRY COMMUNITY AS WELL AS YOUNG EMERGING POETS,
USING THE CULTURAL VISIBILITY OF CITY LIGHTS TO BRING
THEIR WORK TO A WIDER AUDIENCE. IN DOING SO, WE ALSO
HOPE TO DRAW ATTENTION TO THOSE SMALL PRESSES
PUBLISHING SUCH AUTHORS. WITH CITY LIGHTS SPOTLIGHT,
WE WILL MAINTAIN OUR STANDARD OF INNOVATION AND
INCLUSIVENESS BY PUBLISHING HIGHLY ORIGINAL POETRY
FROM ACROSS THE CULTURAL SPECTRUM, REFLECTING
OUR LONGSTANDING COMMITMENT TO THIS MOST
ANCIENT AND STUBBORNLY ENDURING FORM OF ART.

CITY LIGHTS SPOTLIGHT